MOVIE SONGS FOR TWO

Arrangements by Mark Phillips

ISBN 978-1-5400-3720-6

Visit Hal Leonard Online at
www.halleonard.com

Contact us:
Hal Leonard
7777 West Bluemound Road
Milwaukee, WI 53213
Email: info@halleonard.com

In Europe, contact:
Hal Leonard Europe Limited
42 Wigmore Street
Marylebone, London, W1U 2RN
Email: info@halleonardeurope.com

In Australia, contact:
Hal Leonard Australia Pty. Ltd.
4 Lentara Court
Cheltenham, Victoria, 3192 Australia
Email: info@halleonard.com.au

BABY ELEPHANT WALK

from the Paramount Picture HATARI!

VIOLINS

By HENRY MANCINI

Moderately, with humor

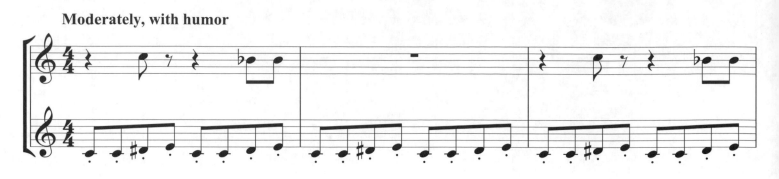

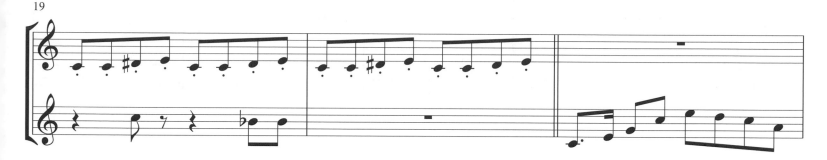

THE CANDY MAN

from WILLY WONKA AND THE CHOCOLATE FACTORY

VIOLINS

Words and Music by LESLIE BRICUSSE
and ANTHONY NEWLEY

CITY OF STARS

from LA LA LAND

VIOLINS

Music by JUSTIN HURWITZ
Lyrics by BENJ PASEK and JUSTIN PAUL

8

CUPS
(When I'm Gone)
from the Motion Picture Soundtrack PITCH PERFECT

VIOLINS

Words and Music by A.P. CARTER,
LUISA GERSTEIN and HELOISE TUNSTALL-BEHRTENS

Moderately fast

FOOTLOOSE

Theme from the Paramount Motion Picture FOOTLOOSE

VIOLINS

Words by DEAN PITCHFORD
Music by KENNY LOGGINS

HALLELUJAH

featured in the DreamWorks Motion Picture SHREK

Words and Music by
LEONARD COHEN

VIOLINS

Moderately slow, in 2

HAPPY

from DESPICABLE ME 2

Words and Music by
PHARRELL WILLIAMS

VIOLINS

I WILL ALWAYS LOVE YOU

featured in THE BODYGUARD

VIOLINS

Words and Music by
DOLLY PARTON

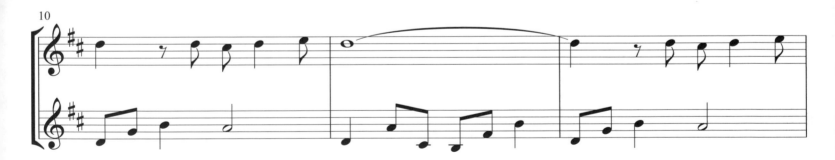

JAILHOUSE ROCK

from JAILHOUSE ROCK

VIOLINS

Words and Music by JERRY LEIBER
and MIKE STOLLER

Moderately fast Rock

MIA & SEBASTIAN'S THEME

from LA LA LAND

VIOLINS

Music by JUSTIN HURWITZ

MRS. ROBINSON

from THE GRADUATE

VIOLINS

Words and Music by
PAUL SIMON

D.S. al Coda

CODA

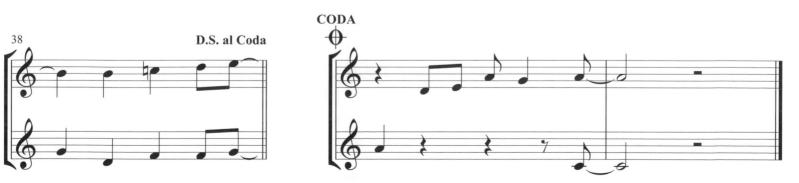

MOON RIVER

from the Paramount Picture BREAKFAST AT TIFFANY'S

VIOLINS

Words by JOHNNY MERCER
Music by HENRY MANCINI

Moderately

THE PINK PANTHER

from THE PINK PANTHER

By HENRY MANCINI

Violins

Moderately, in 4

PUTTIN' ON THE RITZ

from the Motion Picture PUTTIN' ON THE RITZ
featured in YOUNG FRANKENSTEIN

VIOLINS

Words and Music by
IRVING BERLIN

THE RAINBOW CONNECTION

from THE MUPPET MOVIE

VIOLINS

Words and Music by PAUL WILLIAMS
and KENNETH L. ASCHER

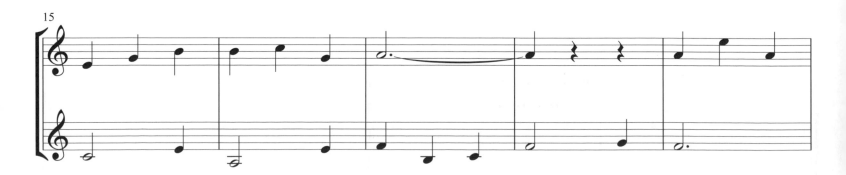

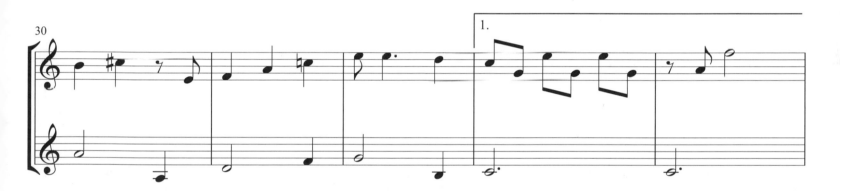

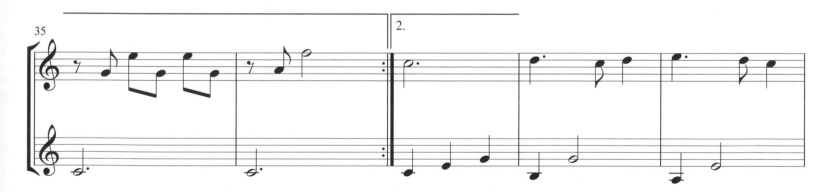

RAINDROPS KEEP FALLIN' ON MY HEAD

from BUTCH CASSIDY AND THE SUNDANCE KID

VIOLINS

Lyrics by HAL DAVID
Music by BURT BACHARACH

ROCK AROUND THE CLOCK

featured in the Motion Picture AMERICAN GRAFFITI
featured in the Motion Picture BLACKBOARD JUNGLE

VIOLINS

Words and Music by MAX C. FREEDMAN
and JIMMY DeKNIGHT

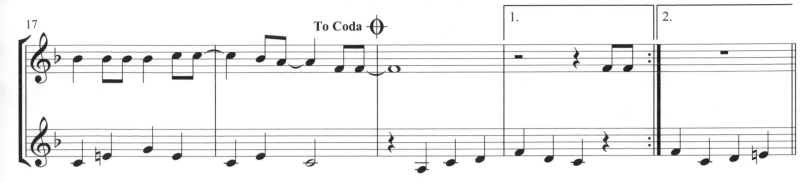

SKYFALL

from the Motion Picture SKYFALL

VIOLINS

Words and Music by ADELE ADKINS
and PAUL EPWORTH

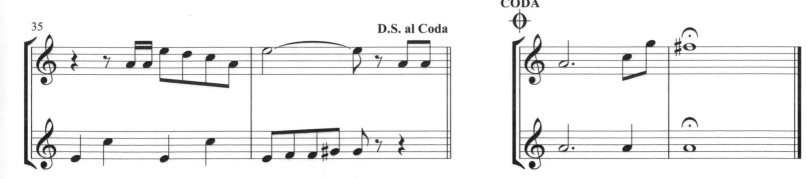

STAYIN' ALIVE

from the Motion Picture SATURDAY NIGHT FEVER

VIOLINS

Words and Music by BARRY GIBB,
ROBIN GIBB and MAURICE GIBB

Moderately, in 2

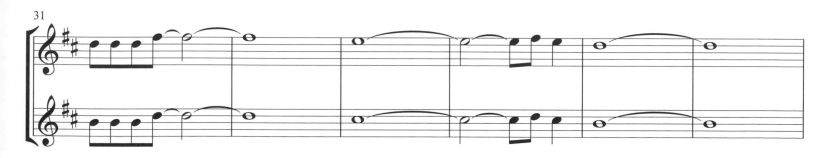

THAT'S AMORÉ
(That's Love)

from the Paramount Picture THE CADDY
featured in the Motion Picture MOONSTRUCK
featured in ENCHANTED

Words by JACK BROOKS
Music by HARRY WARREN

VIOLINS

TIME WARP
from THE ROCKY HORROR PICTURE SHOW

VIOLINS

Words and Music by
RICHARD O'BRIEN

Fast Rock

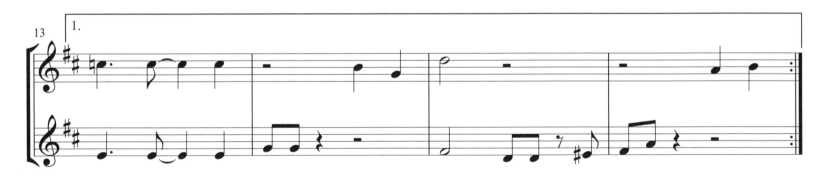

UNCHAINED MELODY

from the Motion Picture UNCHAINED
featured in the Motion Picture GHOST

VIOLINS

Lyric by HY ZARET
Music by ALEX NORTH

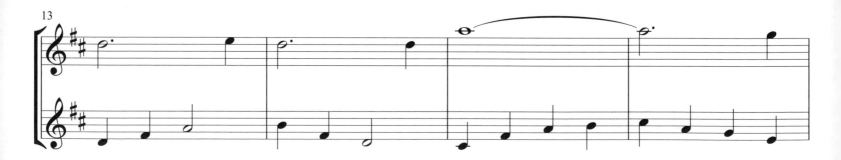

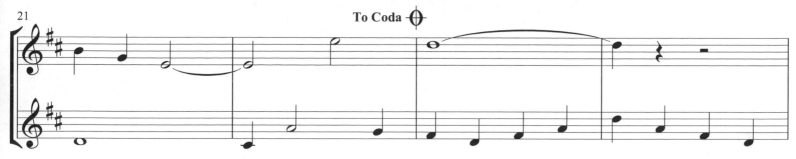

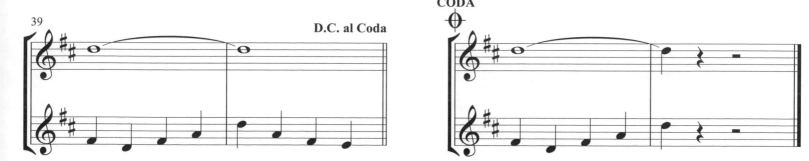

YOU LIGHT UP MY LIFE

from YOU LIGHT UP MY LIFE

VIOLINS

Words and Music by
JOSEPH BROOKS